AF701371

QUESTIONS AND ANSWERS ON THE RULES OF THE ROAD

Page 12.

Page 12.

QUESTIONS AND ANSWERS

on the

RULES OF THE ROAD

For Renewal of Merchant Marine Deck Officers' Licenses and as a Guide for Mariners and Yachtsmen

By

LIEUT. ROBERT J. ZARUBA, USN

CMP

CORNELL MARITIME PRESS, INC.

Cambridge Maryland

1970

ISBN 0-87033-153-1

Library of Congress Catalog Card Number: 73-122248

Printed in the United States of America

"Forehandedness, Vigilance,
and Sound Judgement,
The Price of Safety"

CONTENTS

PREFACE

The officer in charge of the navigation of a vessel is responsible for the safety of the vessel and all who are aboard. Many of his decisions for the safe navigation of the vessel will be governed by following the applicable Rules of the Road. In these situations, the officer in charge will have to rely on his positive knowledge of the Rules, and the responsibilities and burdens they impose, in order to take the action required to avoid disaster. Consequently, a prime requisite for an officer in charge of a vessel's navigation is an absolute knowledge of the Rules of the Road. The officer on the bridge of a vessel, with another vessel rapidly closing on a collision course, cannot afford to be searching books or his memory for a half-remembered rule before deciding on the correct course of action to follow. He must, therefore, maintain such a thorough understanding of the Rules and proper application of their principles that his actions will be intuitively correct from both a legal and seamanlike point of view. The complexity of the International and Inland Rules of the Road, with their attendant similarities and differences, makes their frequent study both desirable and necessary.

Conscientious mariners know that the safety of their own vessel, those around them, as well as their professional reputation, is dependent upon this knowledge. The very purpose in formulating the Rules—the prevention of collision—is a clear indication of the importance which should be given to their study. Unfortunately, in spite of all that has been said and written about the Rules and the clear requirement for certain understanding of their usage, collisions continue to occur in ever increasing numbers because of their violation. Indeed, in an overwhelming number of ship collisions, the primary cause is either careless disregard of the Rules or failure to recall and fulfill the basic action required by them. Many of these tragic disasters could thus have been avoided if only the personnel involved had correctly applied the applicable Rules of the Road.

The maritime community has long realized that one of the continuing requirements for a professional mariner should be a frequent refresher exercise on the Rules of the Road. The meaning of the Rules, the duties and responsibilities they assign in different situations, and the definite actions they require to fulfill their purpose, need to be reviewed regularly by all concerned with the navigation of ships. While there are certain procedures required by the Rules that become routine through frequent usage at sea, there are other facets of Rules which are rarely used and, consequently, almost forgotten by many officers. Nevertheless, the requirement for instant recognition of seldom-seen lights and rarely-heard fog signals is as compulsory as for those routinely seen and heard on every voyage. When such unfamiliar events occur, it is essential that proper action be taken and the correct procedures followed in order to avoid unfortunate incidents. As experience alone will not keep one adequately trained for such emergencies, the conscientious officer should endeavor to prepare himself for all possible circumstances by regularly reviewing the Rules of the Road that are applicable to the waters in which his vessel sails. Self-examination has proved to be a very effective method for refreshing the memory concerning the various phases of the different regulations. Such a refresher exercise is presented in this handbook.

INTRODUCTION

The United States Coast Guard recognized the need to oblige all deck officers to remain familiar with the Rules of the Road, applicable to the waters for which they are licensed, when they amended the regulations for license renewal which became effective on 1 January 1961. Consequently, applicants for merchant marine license renewal must now demonstrate continued proficiency in the Rules before being issued a new license.

This handbook is printed for one purpose, to help the deck officer review for the renewal of his license. The questions printed in this handbook are almost identical to the questions used by Marine Inspectors. Answers to the questions are included but, for better understanding and retention purposes, it is recommended that the officer consult the applicable rule referred to at the end of each question. All applicable rules are taken from Rules of the Road, CG-169.

RULES OF THE ROAD
International – Inland
CG-169
September 1, 1965

Are available from the nearest Marine Inspection Office of the U. S. Coast Guard. See pages 43 through 45 for address of nearest office.

NOTE TO THE YACHTSMAN

Although this handbook was specifically printed to help the Merchant Marine Deck Officer review for the renewal of his deck license, the material is of equal importance to the yachtsman. Regardless of the size of the craft, he is the captain, and just as responsible for the safety of life at sea as the mate or master of a merchant vessel.

To the man in charge of his craft a collision situation is not the time or the place to refer to a reference book. It is his responsibility to be thoroughly familiar with, and to understand, the Rules of the Road situations applicable to the waters on which he may sail. Before getting his craft underway he should review this material. This handbook of questions and answers, with reference to the applicable rule in U.S. Coast Guard Publication 169, will help clarify the Rules of the Road situations.

ACKNOWLEDGMENTS

In preparing this handbook, I have relied on material from the United States Coast Guard and United States Naval Oceanographic offices which contributes to maritime safety. Illustrations of Boundary Lines reprinted by permission from Farwell's Rules of the Nautical Road, 4th Edition, copyright 1968, United States Naval Institute.

Credit is also acknowledged to the United States Coast Guard, Marine Inspection, for their assistance and a "thank you" to my wife for proofreading and typing the manuscript.

The opinions or assertions contained herein are the private ones of the writer and are not to be construed as official or reflecting the views of the Navy Department or the naval service at large.

REQUIREMENTS FOR THE RENEWAL OF MERCHANT MARINE LICENSES

The first category consists of those officers who have not served under the authority of their licenses during the three years next preceding the date of application for renewal, or who have not been employed in a position closely related to the operation of vessels during the same three-year period. As in the past, these officers will be required to pass an examination on the applicable Rules of the Road before their licenses will be renewed.

The second category consists of those officers who have served under the authority of their licenses during the three years next preceding the date of application for renewal, or who have been employed in a position closely related to the operation of vessels during the same three-year period. These officers may renew their licenses in the same manner as in the past, except that each officer must submit an affidavit that he has read within the three months next preceding the date of application for renewal the Rules of the Road applicable to the waters for which he is licensed, and demonstrate his knowledge of the application of such Rules of the Road.

For the officers of the second category, the demonstration of knowledge of the application of the Rules of the Road will consist of an exercise, not an examination. The exercise will be educational in principle and will not be used to create a hardship nor discriminate against any officer at the time of license renewal. The exercise for all deck officers of the second category will be conducted as follows:

(1) Every officer will answer one set of 25 multiple-choice type questions each on the Rules of the Road applicable to the waters for which he is licensed. Should the applicant hold a license where more than one set of Rules of the

Road apply, such as an officer who holds a license on oceans, he shall answer a set of 25 questions on the International Rules of the Road and a set of 25 questions on the Inland and Pilot Rules of the Road.

(2) There are presently two sets of multiple-choice type questions which may be given for the International Rules of the Road exercise and two sets of questions for the Inland and Pilot Rules of the Road exercise. The choice of which set of questions the applicant will receive will be at the discretion of the Officer in Charge, Marine Inspection. Complete details on the requirements for renewal of license are contained in U. S. Coast Guard Navigation and Vessel Inspection Circular No. 7-65.

INTERNATIONAL FLAGS AND PENNANTS
WITH MORSE SYMBOLS

ALPHABET FLAGS			NUMERAL PENNANTS
Alfa .- Have diver down, keep clear	**Kilo** -.- Wish to communicate	**Uniform** ..- You are running into danger	1 .----
Bravo -... Dangerous goods	**Lima** .-.. Stop instantly	**Victor** ...- Require assistance	2 ..---
Charlie -.-. Yes	**Mike** -- Vessel stopped, making no way	**Whis-key** .-- Require medical assistance	3 ...--
Delta -.. Keep clear, maneuvering with difficulty	**Novem-ber** -. No	**Xray** -..- Stop your intentions, watch for signals	4 ....-
Echo . Altering course to starboard	**Oscar** --- Man overboard	**Yankee** -.-- Dragging my anchor	5 .....
Foxtrot ..-. Disabled, communicate with me	**Papa** .--. In harbor–All persons report on board. At sea–Fishing: Nets on obstruction	**Zulu** --.. Require a tug. Fishing: Shooting nets	6 -....
Golf --. Require a pilot. Fishing: Hauling nets	**Quebec** --.- Request free pratique	SUBSTITUTES 1st Substitute	7 --...
Hotel .... Pilot on board	**Romeo** .-. *	2nd Substitute	8 ---..
India .. Altering course to port	**Sierra** ... Engines going astern	3rd Substitute	9 ----.
Juliett .--- On fire, have dangerous cargo, keep clear	**Tango** - Keep clear, engaged in pair trawling	CODE (Answering Pennant or Decimal Point)	0 -----

2d Edition, October 1969

* ONLY used as a Procedure Signal meaning, "Received" or "I have received your last signal" —NOT to be used as a Single Letter Signal.

H.O. MISC. 16539

BOUNDARY LINES

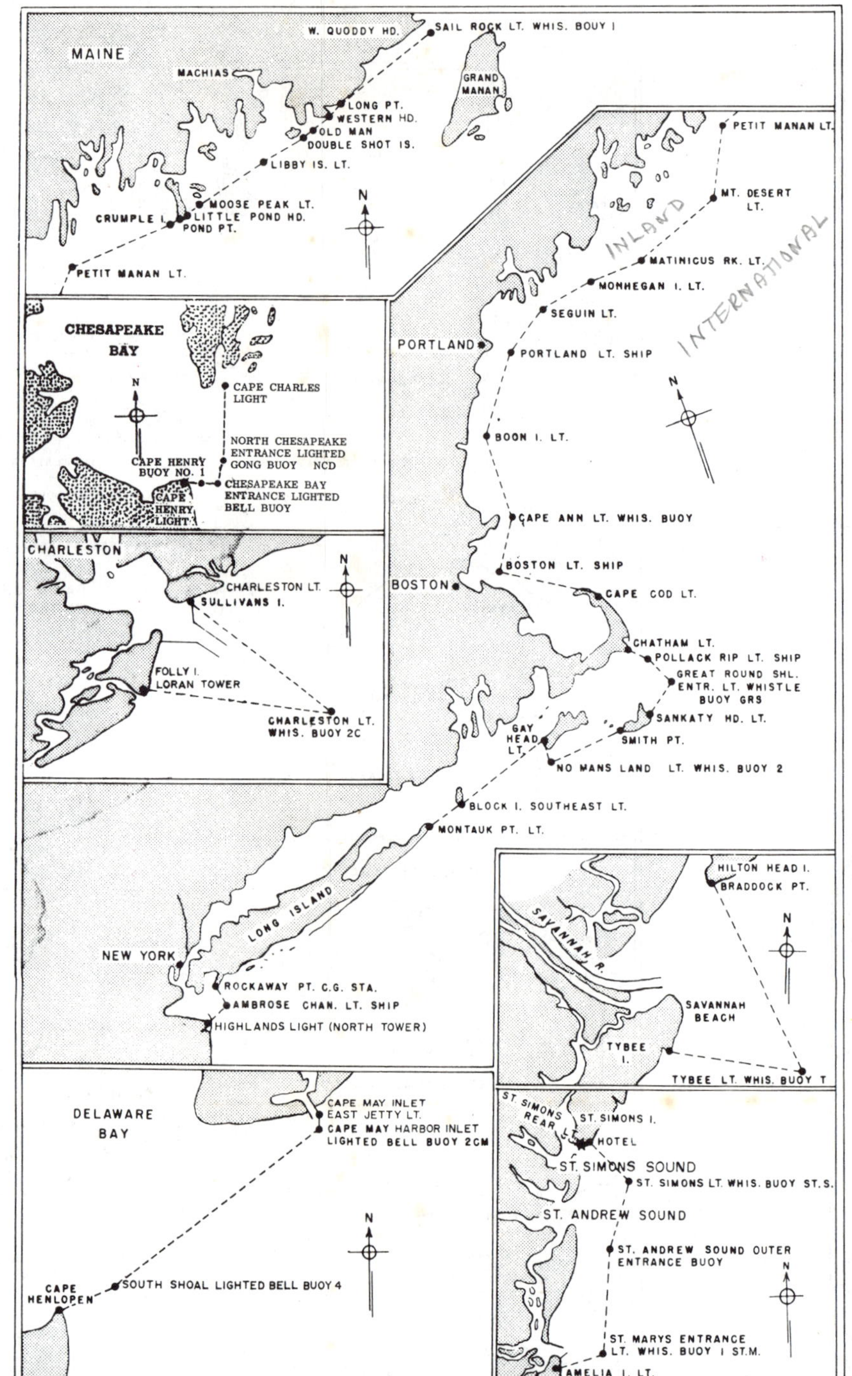

Fig. 1. Boundary lines of inland waters, Atlantic coast of the United States.

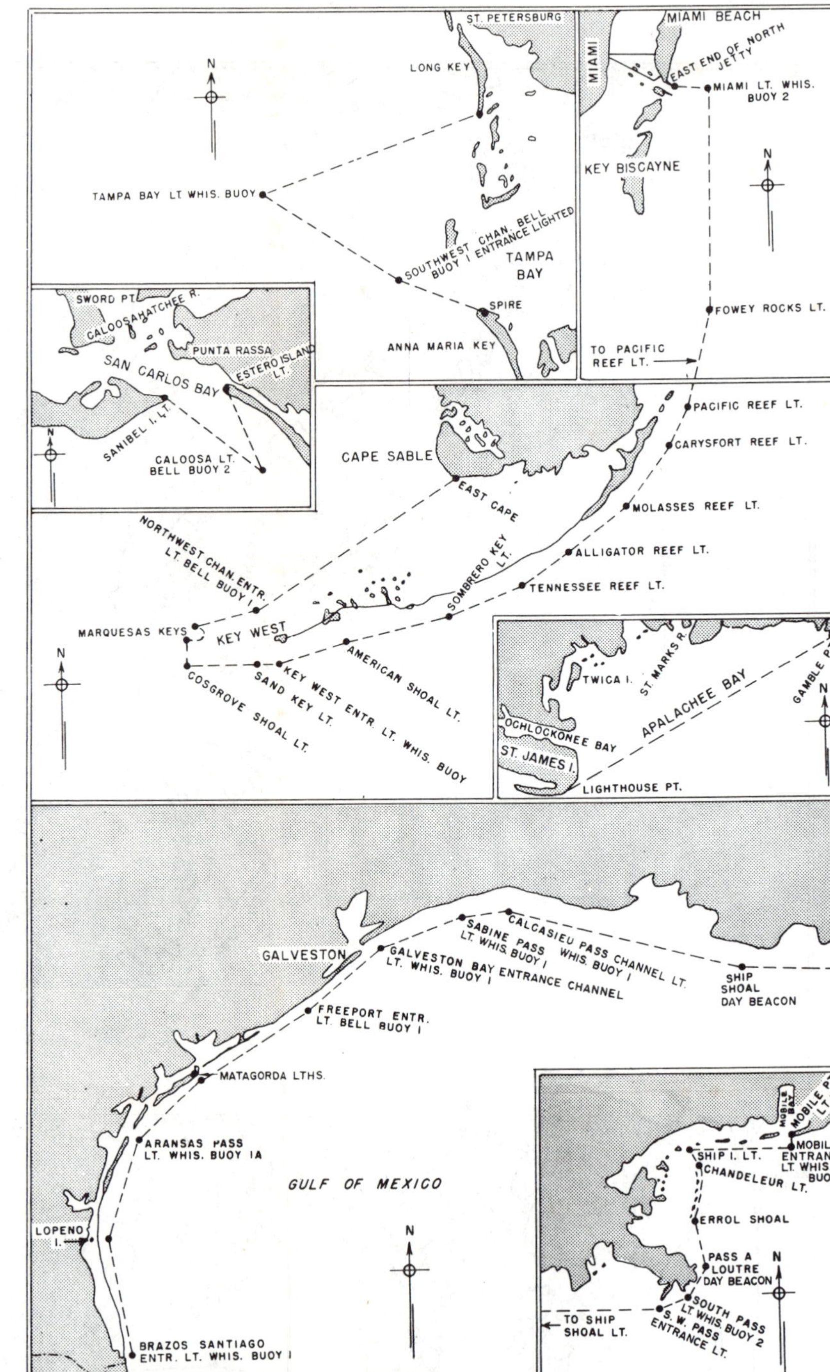

Fig. 2. Boundary lines of inland waters, Gulf coast of the United States.

(See other side for Figures 3, 4, and 5.)

BOUNDARY LINES

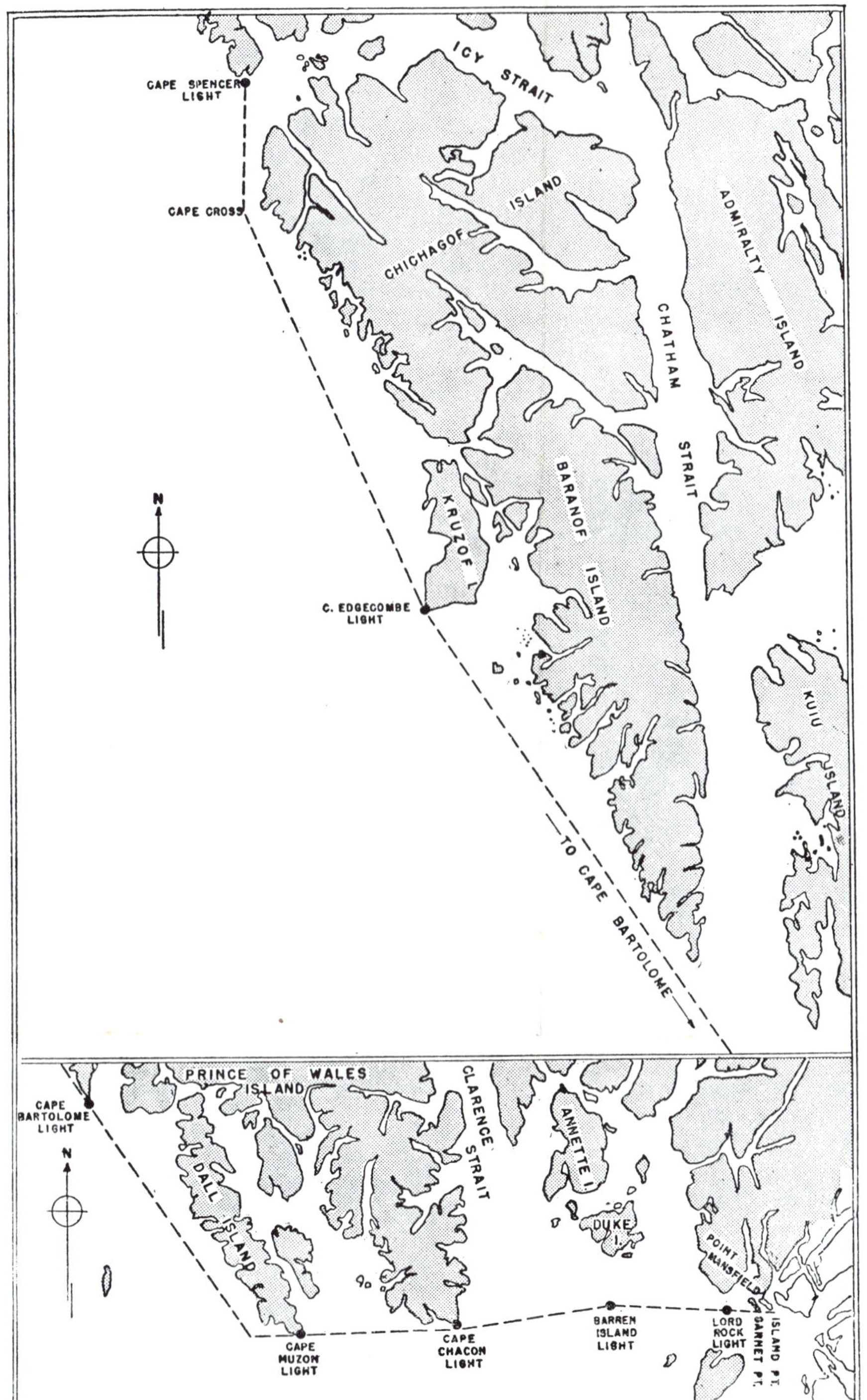

FIG. 5. Boundary line of inland waters, coast of Alaska.

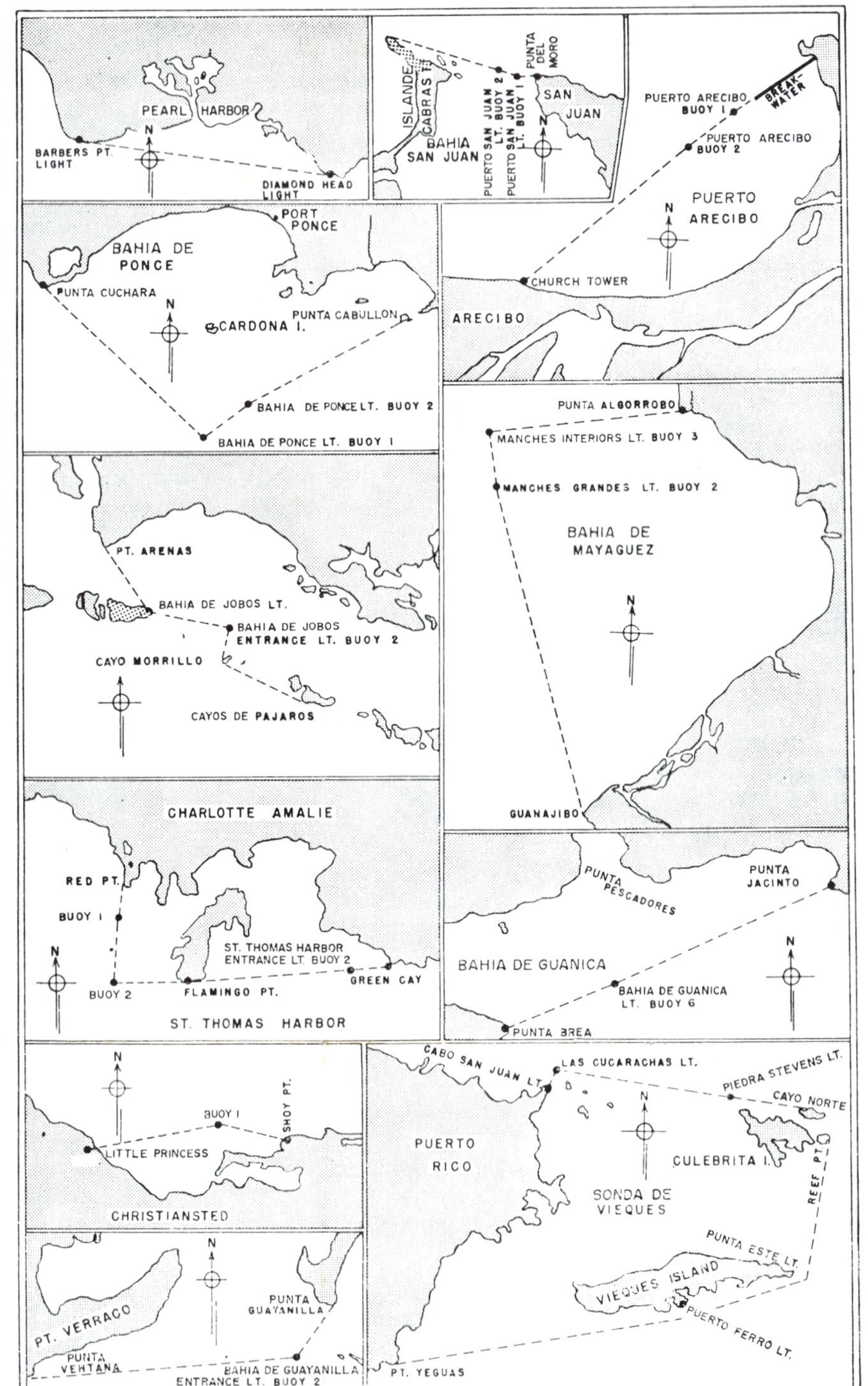

FIG. 4. Boundary lines of inland waters, Hawaii, Puerto Rico, and Virgin Islands.

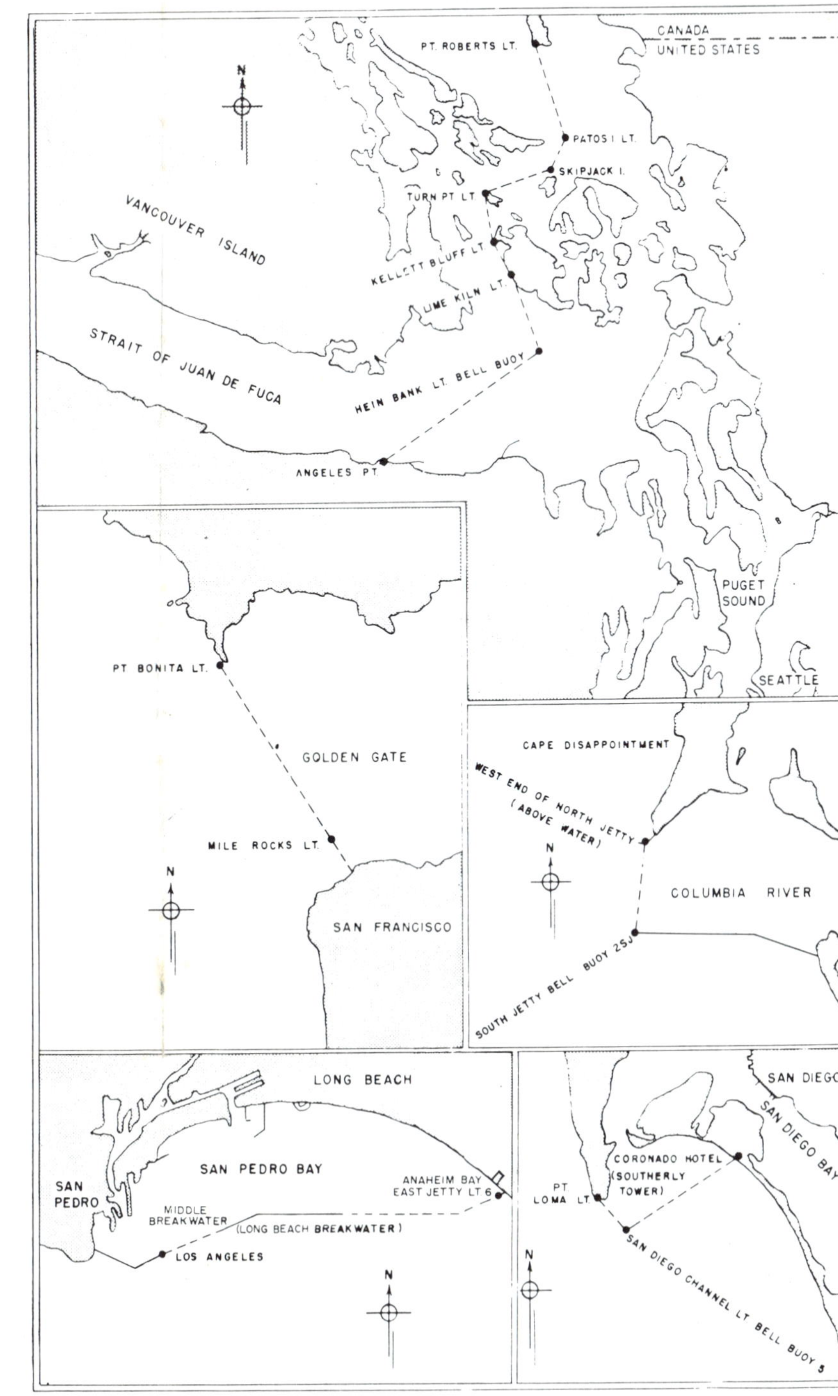

FIG. 3. Boundary lines of inland waters, Pacific coast of the United States.

Part I

BOUNDARY LINES

The purpose of boundary lines is prescribed to establish the lines dividing the high seas from rivers, harbors, and inland waters. The waters inshore of the lines shown in Figures 1, 2, 3, 4 and 5 are "inland waters," and upon them the Inland and Pilot Rules apply. The waters outside of the lines described in the above figures are the "high seas," and upon them the International Rules apply.

Figures 1-5 and International Flags and Pennants with Morse Symbols are on insert facing page 2.

Part II

INTERNATIONAL RULES OF THE ROAD

The term "International Rules of the Road," also referred to as the "International Regulations for Preventing Collisions at Sea," means the rules must be followed by all public and private vessels of the United States (including motorboats) and all water-borne aircraft of the United States navigating upon the high seas. Such regulations shall not apply to the harbors, rivers, and other inland waters of the United States; to the Great Lakes of North America and their connecting and tributary waters as far East as the lower exit of the Saint Lambert Lock at Montreal in the Province of Quebec, Canada; to the Red River of the North and the rivers emptying into the Gulf of Mexico and their tributaries; nor with respect to aircraft in any territorial waters of the United States.

QUESTIONS ON THE

INTERNATIONAL RULES OF THE ROAD

Set No. 1

1. A vessel is underway when:
   (a) She is at anchor
   (b) She is aground
   (c) She is made fast to shore
   (d) She is none of the above

(See Rule 1)

2. Vessel "A":
   (a) Can continue on course and speed
   (b) Must alter course to left
   (c) Must alter course to right
   (d) Must back down

(See Rule 18(a))

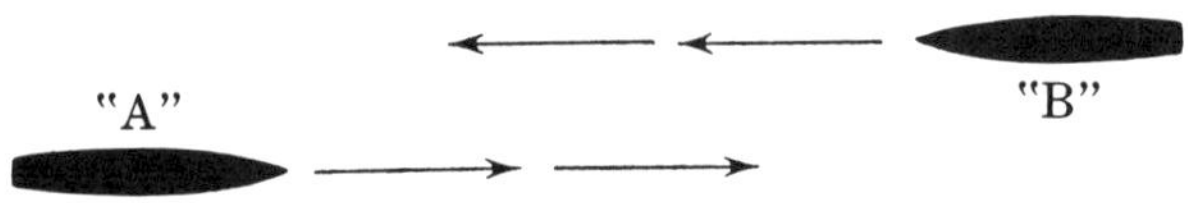

3. If in overtaking another vessel as sketched, you occasionally saw her mast lights and green side light:
   (a) The other vessel must keep clear of you
   (b) You and the other vessel share equally the responsibility for keeping clear
   (c) You should assume that it is your duty to keep clear

(See Rule 24)

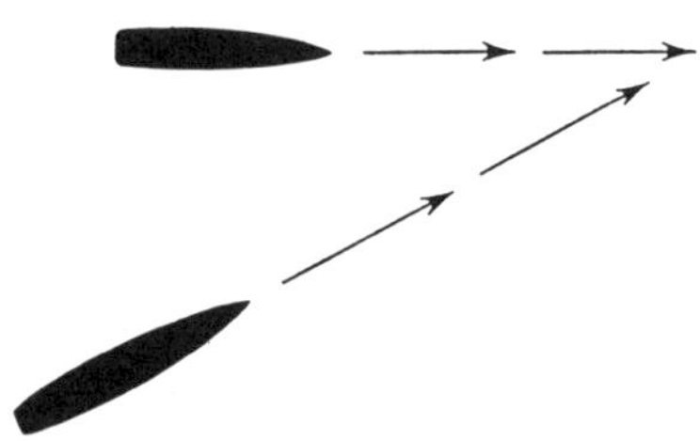

4. At different times, vessel "X" was navigated with respect to the vessels sketched. Which one was she obligated to give way to?
(a) "A" ("A" has overtaken "X")
(b) "B"
(c) "C"
(d) "D" ("X" is overtaking "D")
(See Rule 24)

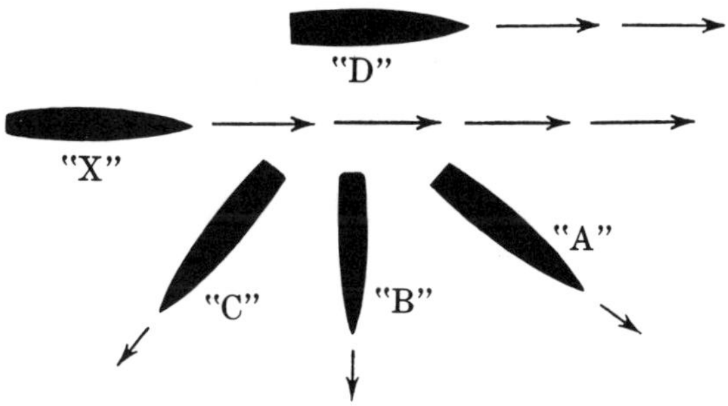

5. At different times, vessel "X" was navigated with respect to the vessels sketched. Which one was she obligated to give way to?
(a) "A"
(b) "B"("B" is overtaking "X")
(c) "C"("C" is overtaking "X")
(d) "D"

(See Rule 24)

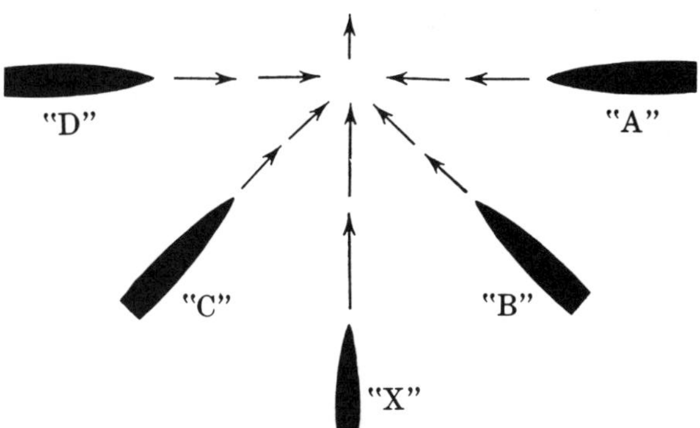

6. The day signal of a basket is displayed by:
   (a) Dredges
   (b) Vessels less than 65 feet in length engaged in fishing
   (c) Cable layers
   (d) Vessels more than 65 feet in length engaged in fishing

(See Rule 9(h))

7. A sailing vessel, of 40 feet or more in length, underway makes her fog signal on a:
   (a) Bell
   (b) Gong
   (c) Whistle
   (d) Fog horn

(See Rule 15(a) (b) (ii))

8. In a narrow channel, power-driven vessels shall, whenever it is safe and practicable:
   (a) Stay in the middle
   (b) Keep to the left
   (c) Keep to the right

(See Rule 25(a))

9. Which of the circles sketched has a white sector showing the arc of visibility of a stern light?

(See Rule 10(a))

"A" "B" "C" "D"

10. On each of the vessels towed at night, as sketched, you should see, looking from abeam:
   (a) A green light
   (b) A red light
   (c) A masthead light
   (d) A forward white light

(See Rule 5(a))

11. A vessel proceeding under sail displaying the black day signal sketched should be regarded as a power-driven vessel.

(a) True
(b) False

(See Rule 14)

12. If you sighted the towboat sketched at night you should see, looking from abeam:

(a) Two white lights in a vertical line and a red side light
(b) Three white lights in a vertical line
(c) A red side light
(d) Three white lights in a vertical line and a red side light

(See Rule 3(a))

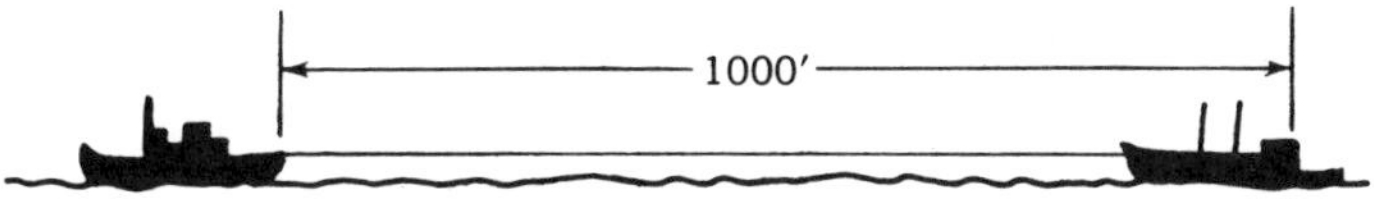

13. In fog, a power-driven vessel, hearing forward of the beam another vessel, the position of which is not ascertained, shall so far as the circumstances of the case admit:

(a) Put the engines on standby
(b) Reduce to one-half speed
(c) Reduce to slow speed
(d) Stop her engines

(See Rule 16(b))

14. In fog, a bell forward and a gong aft must be sounded by anchored vessels whose length is over:

(a) 200 feet
(b) 250 feet
(c) 300 feet
(d) 350 feet

(See Rule 15(iv))

15. Whistle signals to denote course changes must be sounded:

(a) In fog
(b) When vessels are in sight of one another
(c) When you can be reasonably sure of hearing the other vessel's acknowledgment
(d) Every time you alter course

(See Rule 28(a))

16. One of the following statements is correct if "A" and "B" are in sight of one another:

(a) "A" and "B" should each alter course to the right, each blowing one short blast on the whistle
(b) "A" and "B" should each alter course to the right; no whistle signals need be sounded
(c) "A" and "B" should blow one blast and wait for a response before altering course

(See Rule 18 and Rule 28)

17. Approaching an anchorage in fog, you hear one short, one prolonged, and one short blast in that sequence on a ship's whistle. This indicates:

(a) A vessel towing
(b) A vessel not under command
(c) An anchored vessel warning you of her position
(d) A vessel just getting underway from the anchorage
(e) A vessel stopped

(See Rule 15(iv))

18. Vessels towed make fog signals on:

(a) Fog horn or whistle
(b) Whistle only
(c) Fog horn only
(d) Bell
(e) Gong

(See Rule 15(b) (iii))

19. Match each fog signal with the vessel which would sound it:

Signals:

____(a) One prolonged blast on whistle
____(b) One prolonged and two short blasts on the whistle
____(c) Three blasts on the fog horn
____(d) Two prolonged blasts on the whistle
____(e) One prolonged and three short blasts on the whistle
____(f) One prolonged and two short blasts on the whistle

Ships:

A. Vessel towing
B. Fishing vessel
C. Sailing vessel, wind abaft the beam
D. Power-driven vessel underway
E. Vessel towed
F. Power-driven vessel underway but stopped and making no way through the water

(See Rule 15)

20. Match each fog signal with the vessel which would sound it:

Signals:

____(a) Two blasts on the fog horn
____(b) One prolonged and two short blasts on the whistle
____(c) A rapid ringing of a bell followed by the sounding of a gong
____(d) One prolonged and two short blasts on the whistle
____(e) One blast on the fog horn
____(f) A rapid ringing of the bell preceded and followed by three strokes on the bell

Ships:

A. A sailing vessel on the starboard tack
B. A vessel engaged in fishing when underway or at anchor
C. A vessel aground
D. An anchored vessel over 350' in length
E. A vessel picking up a navigation mark
F. A sailing vessel on the port tack

(See Rule 15)

21. A power-driven vessel, when fishing with trolling lines and underway, shall sound what fog signal?

(a) At intervals of not more than 2 minutes, a prolonged blast
(b) At intervals of not more than 2 minutes, two prolonged blasts
(c) At intervals of not more than 1 minute, one prolonged and two short blasts
(d) At intervals of not more than 1 minute, one blast of the whistle followed by the ringing of a bell

(See Rule 15(viii))

22. Match each of the sound signals given with its proper meaning:

Sound signals:

____(a) One short blast on the whistle
____(b) Two short blasts on the whistle
____(c) Three short blasts on the whistle
____(d) Five or more short and rapid blasts on the whistle

Meaning:

A. I am altering course to port
B. My engines are going astern
C. I am altering course to starboard
D. I am in doubt whether you are taking sufficient action to avert collision

(See Rule 28)

23. Which of the circles shown has a black sector which best shows the arc of visibility of the red side light?

(See Rule 2(v))

24. Match the day signals sketched with the class of vessel denoted:

___ (a) Vessel engaged in fishing, outlying gear extends less than 500 feet horizontally into the seaway (See Rule 9(h))
___ (b) Vessel aground (See Rule 11(e))
___ (c) Vessel at anchor (See Rule 11(c))
___ (d) Vessel not under command (See Rule 4(a))
___ (e) Vessel engaged in replenishment at sea (See Rule 4(c))

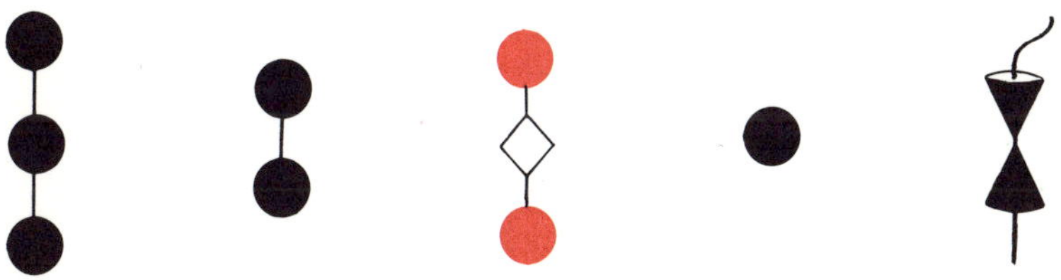

"A" "B" "C" "D" "E"

25. Match the lights sketched with the class of vessel denoted:

___ (a) Vessel engaged in the launching or recovery of aircraft (See Rule 4(c))
___ (b) Power-driven Pilot vessel (See Rule 8(a)(i))
___ (c) Vessel engaged in trawling (See Rule 9(c)(i))
___ (d) Vessel which is not under command (See Rule 4(a))

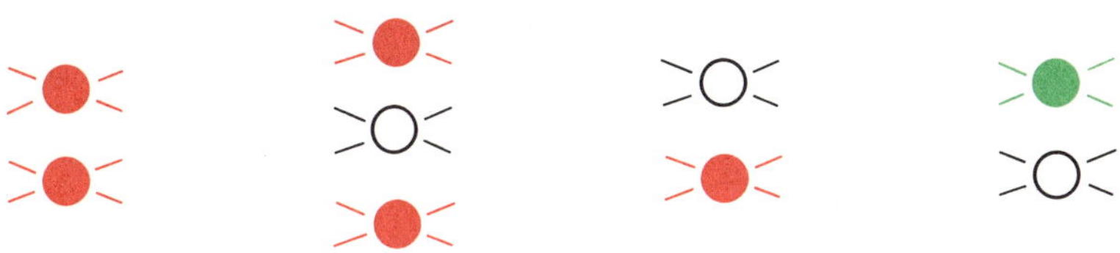

"A" "B" "C" "D"

ANSWERS

Set No. 1

1. d
2. a
3. c
4. d
5. a
6. b
7. d
8. c
9. c
10. b
11. a
12. d
13. d
14. d
15. b
16. a
17. c
18. a
19. D, A, C, F, E, B
20. F, B, D, E, A, C
21. a
22. C, A, B, D
23. c
24. E, A, D, B, C
25. B, C, D, A

QUESTIONS ON THE INTERNATIONAL RULES OF THE ROAD

Set No. 2

1. Vessels are deemed to be in sight of one another only when:

   (a) One is observed from the other either visually or with radar
   (b) One can be observed visually from the other
   (c) There is no fog
   (d) They can be observed on radar screens
   (e) All of the above

(See Rule 1 (ix))

2. The annex of eight principles to the International Rules contains:

   (a) Recommendations to assist in the use of radar
   (b) Amendments to the steering and sailing rules
   (c) Preliminary definitions

(See Annex to Rules)

3. If a close quarters situation is imminent, the most prudent action may be to take all the way off the vessel:

   (a) True (b) False

(See Annex to Rules)

4. The two white lights displayed as sketched would be required and would indicate at night that the vessel is:

   (a) Not under command
   (b) Over 150 feet in length and is at anchor
   (c) Under 150 feet in length and is at anchor
   (d) Aground

(See Rule 11)

5. Vessels not under command shall display their side lights and stern light at all times while underway:
   (a) True (b) False
(See Rule 4(a) (e))

6. The term "short blast" means a blast having a duration of about:
   (a) One second (c) Three seconds
   (b) Two seconds (d) Four seconds
(See Rule 1(xi))

7. If you should hear, while underway in fog, three blasts in succession, namely a short blast, a prolonged blast, and a short blast, it should indicate to you a ________________.
   (a) Vessel towing (c) Vessel towed
   (b) Vessel not under command (d) Vessel at anchor
   (e) Fishing vessel
(See Rule 15(iv))

8. A vessel propelled by both sail and power is considered by the International Rules of the Road to be a sailing vessel:
   (a) True (b) False
(See Rule 1(c) (iv))

9. Which of the following signals would a vessel give simply to attract the attention of another vessel?
   (a) Three short blasts of the whistle
   (b) A flare-up light
   (c) Flames on the vessel
   (d) Two red lights in a vertical line
   (e) A continuous sounding of the whistle
(See Rules 4, 12, 28 and 31)

10. When in sight of another vessel, a power-driven vessel should sound one short blast of the whistle when altering course to starboard:
   (a) True (b) False
(See Rule 28)

11. Every vessel which is directed by these Rules to keep out of the way of another vessel shall, so far as possible, take positive early action to comply with this obligation, and shall, if the circumstances of the case admit, avoid crossing ahead of the other:

(a) True (b) False

(See Rule 22)

12. If you should sight the lights of a towing vessel as sketched, you would know she is towing:

(a) One vessel astern, length of tow less than 600 feet
(b) More than one vessel alongside
(c) By pushing a vessel ahead
(d) One or more than one vessel astern and length of tow exceeds 600 feet
(e) Two vessels astern, length of tow less than 600 feet

(See Rule 3)

13. At night you sight a vessel displaying a green light over a white light on your port beam; you would expect it to be:

(a) A vessel fishing with Trolling lines
(b) A vessel engaged in fishing and not Trawling
(c) A cable laying vessel underway, starboard side to
(d) A cable laying vessel underway, starboard side to
(e) A towing vessel underway

(See Rule 9(c) (i))

Line (d) should read: "A Vessel engaged in Trawling."

14. The International Rules of the Road shall be followed by all vessels and seaplanes:

(a) Upon international waters only
(b) Upon the high seas and all inland waters

(c) Upon the high seas and in all waters connected therewith navigable by seagoing vessels, except as provided in Rule 30
(d) Upon the high seas and all waters connected therewith navigable by seagoing vessels, except the Great Lakes

(See Rule 1)

15. If you should sight the vessel displaying the lights as shown, you would expect it to be:
(a) A vessel fishing with her gear fast to a rock
(b) A vessel aground
(c) An anchored vessel laying cable
(d) A power-driven pilot vessel at anchor

(See Rules 8(a) (i) and 11(a))

16. If you should sight the vessel displaying the lights as shown, you would expect it to be:
(a) A fishing vessel anchored
(b) A vessel over 150 feet in length aground
(c) A pilot vessel anchored
(d) An anchored vessel laying cable
(e) A vessel underway but not under command

(See Rule 11(e))

17. When a power-driven vessel and a sailing vessel are proceeding so as to involve risk of collision, the power-driven vessel shall keep out of the way except when:
(a) The sailing vessel is crossing from starboard to port
(b) The sailing vessel is crossing from port to starboard
(c) Meeting head and head
(d) Being overtaken by the sailing vessel
(e) The sailing vessel is running free

(See Rule 20(a))

18. If a power-driven vessel sounds two short blasts of the whistle, it signifies:
   (a) Her intention to alter course to port
   (b) That she is altering course to port
   (c) That she intends to overtake and pass a vessel on her starboard side
   (d) A starboard-to-starboard passage in a meeting situation (See Rule 28(a))

19. Whenever a power-driven vessel, which under the Rules is to keep her course and speed, is in sight of another vessel and is in doubt whether sufficient action is being taken by the other vessel to avert collision, she may indicate such doubt by giving at least _______ short and rapid blasts of the whistle:
   (a) 2 (b) 3 (c) 4 (d) 5
   (See Rule 28(b))

20. At sea you sight through binoculars a vessel ahead displaying the signal sketched from the triatic stay. You should _________:

   (a) Stay clear, as the vessel is not under command
   (b) Stay clear, as it is a cable layer
   (c) Render assistance, for the vessel is in distress
   (d) Dip your ensign when passing, for it is a man-of-war (See Rule 31(a) (vii))

21. The General Prudential Rule would apply when meeting all but one of the following. To which one would it not apply?
   (a) When more than one vessel is crossing your course on opposite headings
   (b) When meeting a tug with a tow navigating in a strong current
   (c) When meeting a vessel that is unable to maneuver in accordance with the rules
   (d) When encountering a vessel engaged in laying a cable
   (e) When a course change does not appear necessary in meeting a vessel starboard-to-starboard
   (See Rule 27)

22. At sea, you are on a power-driven vessel underway and making way in dense fog. The visibility is approximately one-third of a mile. You hear a fog signal of another vessel apparently forward of your beam and observe her in the radar screen three points on the port bow, one mile distant. You put your engines full speed astern and simultaneously sound the whistle. Which of the following would be the correct signal?

(a) Five or more short and rapid blasts
(b) A prolonged blast
(c) Two prolonged blasts
(d) Three short blasts to indicate the engines are going astern
(e) A prolonged blast and three short blasts with an interval between

(See Rules 15 and 28(a))

23. At night, if you should sight the vessel displaying the lights as shown, you would expect it to be:

(a) A vessel engaged in fishing
(b) A pilot vessel underway on station
(c) A vessel fishing with Trolling lines
(d) A cable-laying vessel underway, portside to
(e) A vessel engaged in Trawling

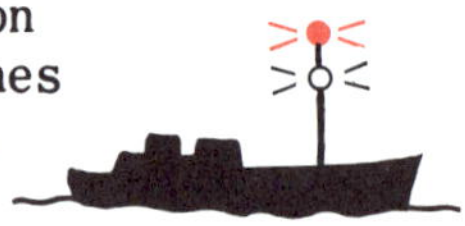

(See Rule 9(d))

24. At sea, during the daytime you sight a vessel displaying the black shape consisting of two cones with their points together, as shown, and you identify the vessel as:

(a) A vessel aground in international waters
(b) A vessel over 65 feet in length engaged in fishing
(c) A vessel less than 150 feet in length at anchor
(d) A vessel towing a submerged object
(e) A vessel in distress and requiring assistance

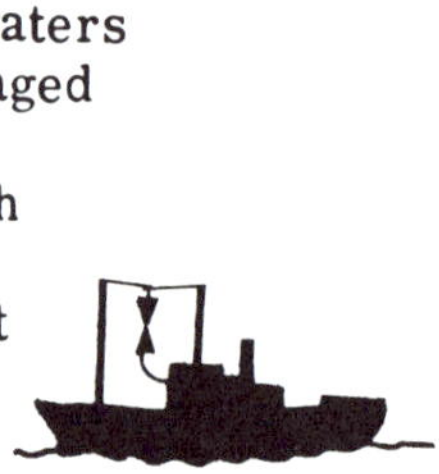

(See Rule 9(h))

25. At night, underway you sight the vessel displaying the lights as shown; you would expect it to be:
   (a) A sail vessel Trawling
   (b) A sail vessel engaged in fishing
   (c) A sailing vessel underway
   (d) A sailing pilot vessel, engaged on pilotage duty, underway
   (e) A sail vessel underway, not under command
(See Rule 5(b))

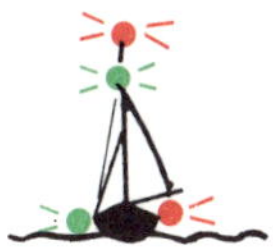

ANSWERS

Set. No. 2

1. b
2. a
3. a
4. b
5. b
6. a
7. d
8. b
9. b
10. a
11. a
12. d
13. d
14. c
15. d
16. b
17. d
18. b
19. d
20. c
21. e
22. b
23. a
24. b
25. c

Part III

INLAND AND PILOT RULES

The term "Inland and Pilot Rules" means that the rules for preventing collisions shall be followed by all vessels upon the harbors, rivers, and other inland waters of the United States, except the Great Lakes and their connecting and tributary waters as far east as Montreal, and the waters of the Mississippi River between its source and the Huey P. Long Bridge and all of its tributaries emptying thereinto and their tributaries and that part of the Atchafalaya River above its junction with the Plaquemina-Morgan City alternate waterway, and the Red River of the North; and are hereby declared special rules duly made by local authority.

QUESTIONS ON THE INLAND AND PILOT RULES

Set No. 1

1. A steam vessel may use a siren sounded by air when giving the prescribed fog signals.

(a) True (b) False

(See Article 15)

2. Sail vessels and vessels towed make fog signals on:

(a) Bell (c) Whistle or fog horn

(b) Gong (d) Whistle only

(e) Fog horn only

(See Article 15)

3. A steam vessel underway in fog, but stopped and having no way upon her, blows on her whistle:

(a) One prolonged blast every two minutes
(b) Two prolonged blasts every two minutes
(c) One prolonged blast every minute
(d) One short blast every minute

(See Article 15)

4. On overtaking another vessel, before passing her on her port side, you must:

(a) Blow one short blast and be answered by one short blast
(b) Blow two short blasts and be answered by two short blasts
(c) Blow one short blast
(d) Blow two short blasts

(See Article 18, Rule VIII)

5. The day signal sketched indicates that the vessel is:

(a) Handling buoys
(b) Anchored
(c) Dredging
(d) Engaged in hydrographic survey

(See Pilot Rule 80. 25)

6. Rowing boats under sail or oars must show:
   (a) Side lights
   (b) Mast lights
   (c) Stern light
   (d) A white light in time to prevent collision

(See Article 7)

7. In fog, an anchored vessel must ring the bell every:
   (a) Minute for five seconds
   (b) Two minutes for five seconds
   (c) Three minutes for ten seconds

(See Article 15)

8. Risk of collision can best be determined by:
   (a) Checking the distance of an approaching vessel
   (b) Carefully watching the compass bearing of an approaching vessel
   (c) Watching the other vessel for any signals she may give
   (d) Observing the range of the approaching vessel's masts or mast light

(See Preliminary to Steering & Sailing Rules)

9. A vessel signifies intention to pass a dredge by blowing:
   (a) One short blast (c) Three short blasts
   (b) Two short blasts (d) One long blast

(See Pilot Rule 80. 26)

10. Passing within 200 feet of floating plants in channels, maximum speed is:
   (a) Three miles per hour (c) Five miles per hour
   (b) Four miles per hour (d) Six miles per hour

(See Pilot Rule 80. 27)

11. "My engines are going full speed astern" is indicated on the whistle by:
   (a) One short blast (c) Three short blasts
   (b) Two short blasts (d) Four short blasts

(See Article 28)

12. If you were in charge of navigation of "A," you should not:

(a) Go under stern of "B"
(b) Back down on engines
(c) Stop
(d) Cross ahead of "B"

(See Article 22)

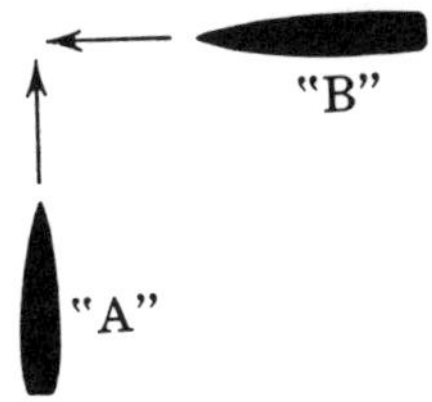

13. If you were in charge of navigation of "B," you should:

(a) Go under stern of "A"
(b) Back down on engines
(c) Stop
(d) Hold course and speed

(See Article 21)

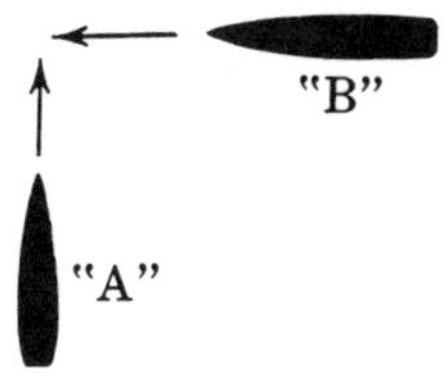

14. When collision cannot be avoided by "A" alone, "B" must:

(a) Cross under "A's" stern
(b) Back down
(c) Hold course and speed under all circumstances
(d) Take such action as will best aid to avert collision

(See Article 27)

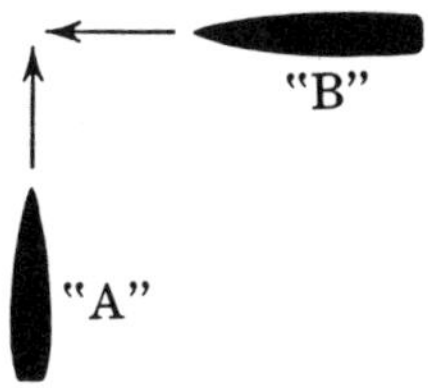

15. If you were in charge of navigation of "A," you should:

(a) Blow one blast
(b) Blow two blasts

(c) Hold course and speed, letting "B" take avoiding action
(d) Stop in all cases

(See Article 18, Rule I)

16. Whistle signals to indicate course changes have a duration of:

(a) One second
(b) Two seconds
(c) Three seconds
(d) Four seconds

(See Pilot Rule 80.03)

17. The Rule of Special Circumstance would apply when meeting all but one of the following. To which one would it not apply?

(a) When meeting several vessels at one time
(b) When meeting a tug with tow bound downstream in a heavy current
(c) When meeting a vessel unable to maneuver in accordance with the Rules
(d) When encountering a vessel engaged in laying cable
(e) When meeting a vessel end-on or nearly end-on

(See Article 27)

18. The two white lights displayed as sketched would indicate at night that:

(a) The vessel is not under command
(b) The vessel is over 150 feet in length and is at anchor
(c) The vessel is fishing
(d) The vessel is under 150 feet and is at anchor

(See Article 11)

19. At different times, vessel "X" was navigated with respect to the four vessels sketched. Which one was obligated to give way to?

(a) "A" ("A" is overtaking "X")
(b) "B"
(c) "C"
(d) "D" ("X" is overtaking "D")
(See Article 24)

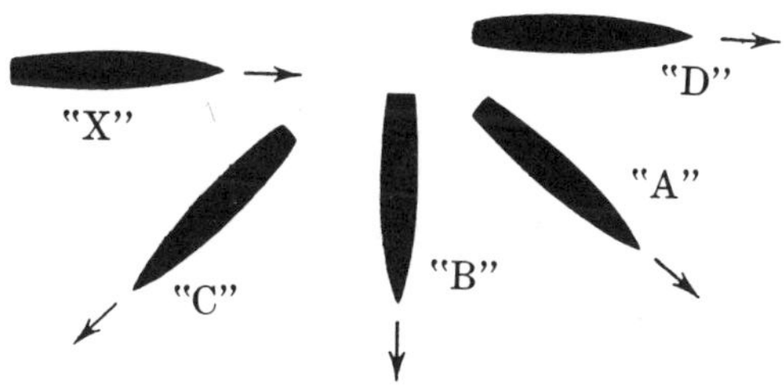

20. Match the fog signals listed with the class of vessel denoted:

___(a) A prolonged blast of the whistle every minute
___(b) A blast of the fog horn every minute
___(c) A rapid ringing of the bell for 5 seconds every minute
___(d) Two blasts of the fog horn every minute
___(e) Three blasts of the fog horn
___(f) One prolonged blast followed by two short blasts on the whistle

A. A steam vessel towing
B. A sailing vessel on the starboard tack
C. A sailing vessel on the port tack
D. A sailing vessel with the wind abaft the beam
E. A steam vessel underway
F. A vessel at anchor
(See Article 25)

21. The two vessels sketched are governed by the ____ rule:

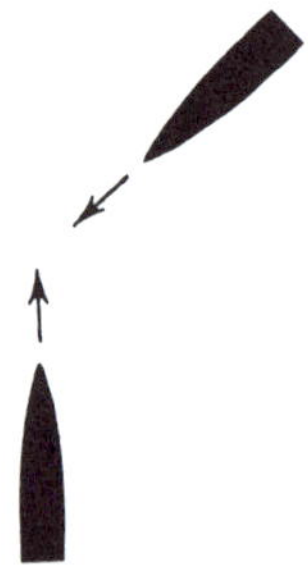

(a) Overtaking
(b) Meeting end-on
(c) Crossing
(d) Approaching

(See Article 19)

22. Nearing a bend, where the channel around the bend is obscured, a vessel should blow on the whistle:

(a) A short blast
(b) A long blast
(c) Two long blasts
(d) Three long blasts

(See Article 18, Rule V)

23. The vessel with lights shown as sketched, seen in inland waters, would be:

(a) Dredging
(b) Laying mats
(c) Fishing
(d) Not under command
(e) A pilot vessel

(See Article 9)

24. The vessel showing lights as sketched would be:

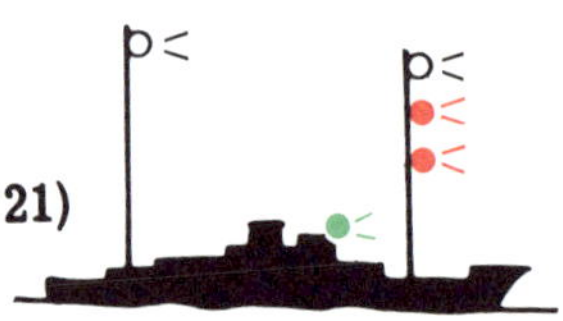

(a) Towing a submerged object
(b) Not under command
(c) A self-propelled suction dredge
(d) Laying telegraph cable

(See Pilot Rule 80. 21)

25. Match the signals sketched with the class of vessel denoted.

__(a) A dredge underway engaged in dredging (See Pilot Rule 80. 21)
__(b) Engaged in hydrographic survey (See Pilot Rule 80. 33)
__(c) Towing a submerged object (See Pilot Rule 80. 18)
__(d) Handling navigation aid (See Pilot Rule 80. 33a)
__(e) Laying cables or pipes (See Pilot Rule 80. 22)

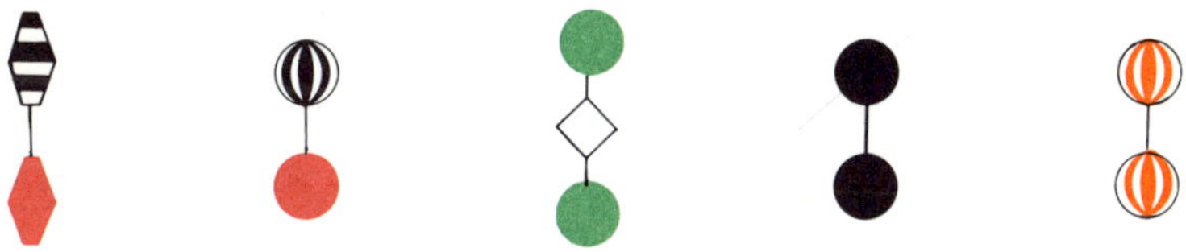

"A" "B" "C" "D" "E"

ANSWERS

Set No. 1

1. a
2. e
3. c
4. b
5. b
6. d
7. a
8. b
9. d
10. c
11. c
12. d
13. d
14. d
15. a
16. a
17. d
18. b
19. d
20. E, B, F, C, D, A
21. c
22. b
23. c
24. c
25. D, C, A, E, B

QUESTIONS ON THE INLAND AND PILOT RULES

Set No. 2

1. You are on vessel "A" and observed vessel "B" four points abaft your starboard beam. The bearing between the two subsequently alters as shown. You are ________.
   (a) Now the burdened vessel in a crossing situation
   (b) Now the privileged vessel in a crossing situation
   (c) Still privileged, as in the original overtaking situation
   (d) Still burdened, as in the original overtaking situation
   (See Article 24 & Pilot Rule 80. 6)

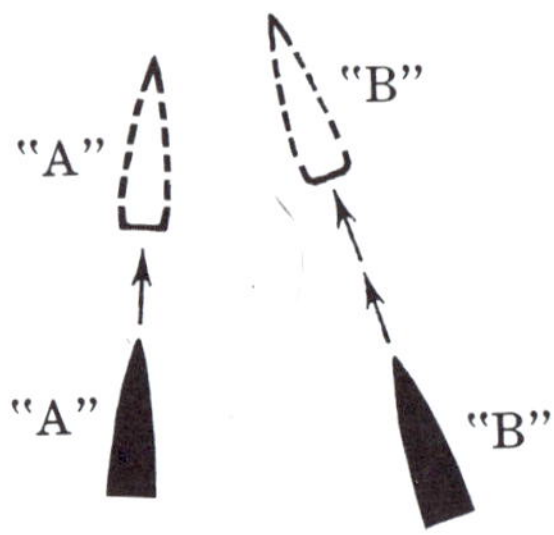

2. A horizontal line of amber lights crossing a channel a short distance above the water often indicates a pipeline.
   (a) True (b) False
   (See Pilot Rule 80. 23)

3. Incorrectly answering a two-blast signal with one blast, or incorrectly answering a one-blast signal with two, is known as:
   (a) Reverse signals (c) Danger signals
   (b) Turned signals (d) Cross signals
   (See Pilot Rule 80. 2)

4. In the situation sketched, one short blast by "A" indicates she is holding course and speed.
   (a) True
   (b) False

(See Pilot Rule ~~80. 3~~) 80.03(a)(3)

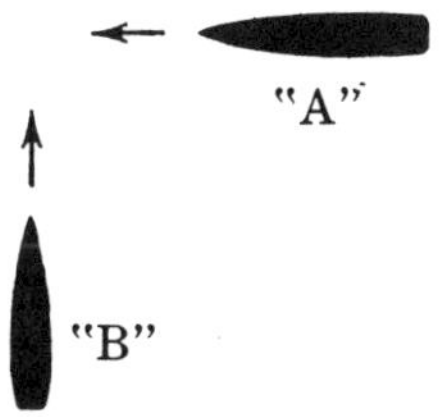

5. You are on vessel "A" which is overtaking vessel "B." You must blow one short blast and be answered by one short blast before attempting to pass..
   (a) True
   (b) False

(See Article 18 & Pilot Rule 80. 6)

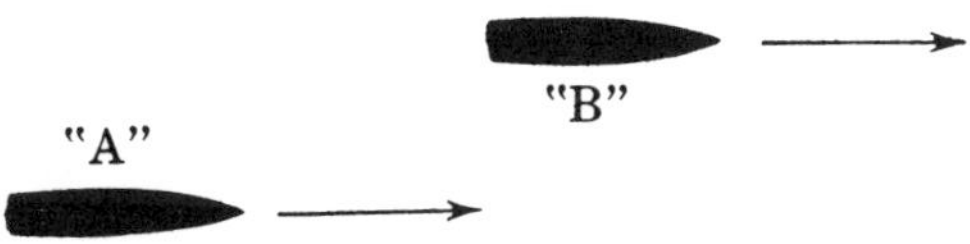

6. At night you see a vessel outside the channel ahead showing a red light over a white light. You next see this vessel extinguish these lights and in lieu thereof, show a single white light. The vessel is probably a:
   (a) Fishing vessel observed from aft and no longer engaged in fishing
   (b) Vessel that was not under command and once again underway
   (c) Steam pilot vessel that has anchored
   (d) Sail vessel that was close hauled on the port tack and now running free

(See Articles 2, 5, 8, and 9)

7. If you should observe from the bridge of your vessel two amber lights in a vertical line with or without a white light above it, you should identify it as ____________.

(a) A Coast Guard vessel servicing an aid to navigation
(b) An opening in a pipeline
(c) A vessel towing by pushing ahead
(d) A dredge held stationary by spuds
(e) A pilot vessel at anchor

(See Articles 3 & 8; also Pilot Rules 80. 20, 80. 23 & 80. 33)

8. When passing a Coast Guard vessel servicing an aid to navigation, speed shall be sufficiently reduced to insure the safety of both vessels, and when passing within 200 feet of the Coast Guard vessel, speed shall not exceed:

(a) 3 miles per hour (c) 5 miles per hour
(b) 4 miles per hour (d) 6 miles per hour

(See Pilot Rule 80. 33a)

9. A vessel which should hold her course and speed in a crossing or overtaking situation is no longer privileged when action by both vessels is necessary to avoid collision.

(a) True (b) False

(See Article 27)

10. Failure to understand the course or intention of an approaching vessel should be indicated by:

(a) One short blast
(b) Three short blasts
(c) Not less than four short and rapid blasts
(d) One long blast

(See Article 18 and Pilot Rule 80. 1)

11. If your one blast signal is answered with two blasts, your next whistle signal should be:

(a) One blast (b) Two blasts
(c) The danger signal

(See Pilot Rules 80. 1 & 80. 2; also Article 18, Rule III)

12. In a narrow channel, power-driven vessels shall whenever safe and practicable stay in the middle.

(a) True (b) False

(See Article 25 and Pilot Rule 80. 10)

13. The vessel sketched is underway at night. From the lights displayed you would know she is:

(a) Engaged in laying cable
(b) Towing a vessel alongside or pushing ahead
(c) Towing one or more vessels astern
(d) A pilot vessel underway on station

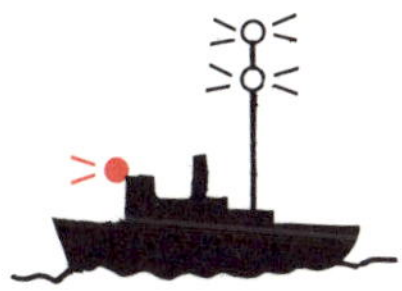

(See Article 3)

14. If you heard a prolonged blast followed by two short blasts given on a fog horn, you should identify it as______.

(a) A steam vessel towing
(b) A sailing vessel running free
(c) A vessel not under command
(d) A steam vessel underway but stopped
(e) A vessel being towed

(See Article 15)

15. Every vessel which is directed by these rules to keep out of the way of another vessel shall always cross ahead of the other.

(a) True (b) False

(See Article 22)

16. A steam vessel about to enter a fog bank hears, apparently forward of her port beam, the fog signal of another vessel the position of which is not ascertained. She shall:

(a) Navigate with caution
(b) Alter course to the left and pass astern of the other vessel
(c) Stop her engines and then navigate with caution
(d) Sound whistle and maintain course and speed
(e) Slow her engines to moderate speed and then navigate with caution

(See Article 16)

17. While passing over the lines of a floating plant working in a channel, a vessel's propelling machinery must be stopped.

(a) True (b) False

(See Pilot Rule 80.27)

18. If the compass bearing of an approaching vessel on your starboard bow changes appreciably to the left, she will pass astern of you.

(a) True (b) False

19. What change should the sketched steam vessel make to her lights if she is broken down and underway at night in inland waters?

(a) Turn off the range lights and hoist two all-around red lights
(b) Hoist two red lights in addition to the lights shown
(c) Put up two additional white lights on the foremast
(d) Make no change as there is none prescribed

(See Article 2)

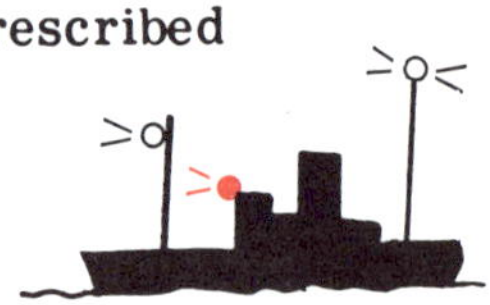

20. Which two of the types of vessels listed would display the sketched black signal during the daytime?

(1) Coast & Geodetic Survey vessel at anchor in a fairway engaged in surveying
(2) Self-propelled suction dredge underway and dredging
(3) A steamer towing a submerged object
(4) A vessel anchored and laying a cable
(5) A dredge held in stationary position by moorings or spuds

(a) Both (1) and (2)
(b) Both (1) and (3)
(c) Both (3) and (5)
(d) Both (2) and (4)

(See Pilot Rules 80.18, 80.20, 80.21, 80.22 and 80.33)

21. A vessel overtaking you blows two short blasts. You think it dangerous for her to pass. You should:
   (a) Blow one prolonged blast followed by two short blasts
   (b) Blow two short blasts
   (c) Blow three short blasts
   (d) Blow four or more short and rapid blasts
   (e) Ignore the signal until you deem it safe for the other vessel to pass
   (See Article 18, Rule VIII & Pilot Rule 80.6)

22. A vessel's engines are put full speed astern while backing from a dock into the channel. If, due to the height of the pier structure, she cannot observe a vessel approaching, she should give as a signal_______of the whistle.
   (a) One long blast
   (b) Three short blasts
   (c) One long blast and three short blasts
   (d) Three short blasts and a prolonged blast
   (See Article 18 and 28 & Pilot Rule 80.5)

23. A class "2" motorboat equipped with lights in accordance with section 3(b) of the motorboat Act of 1940 as amended would carry________.
   (a) 32 point white lights forward and aft, and fixed red and green side lights
   (b) A combined lantern forward showing red and green and a 32 point white light
   (c) A 20 point white light forward, 32 point white light aft, and fixed red and green side lights
   (d) A 32 point white light aft and fixed side lights
   (See excerpts from Act of April 25, 1940)

24. At night your vessel is being moved as a dead ship from one berth to another with the aid of three tugs. What navigation lights shall be displayed on your vessel?
   (a) Masthead, range, side lights and stern light
   (b) Masthead, range, side lights, two red lights in a vertical line and stern light

(c) Two red lights in a vertical line, side lights and stern light
(d) Side lights and stern light
(e) Two red lights in a vertical line
(See Articles 5 and 10)

25. Match the lights sketched with the class of vessel denoted:
___(a) Vessel towing a submerged object with no signal on tow
___(b) Steam pilot vessel underway on station
___(c) Vessel anchored and engaged in laying cable
___(d) Vessel towing one or more vessels astern
(See Articles 3 & 8; also Pilot Rules 80. 18 and 80. 22)

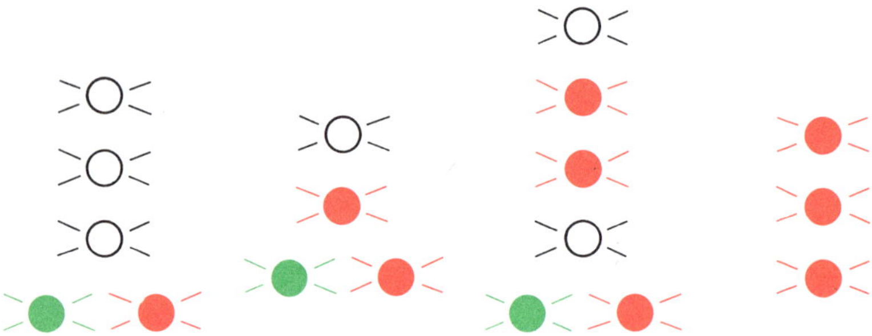

"A" "B" "C" "D"

ANSWERS

Set No. 2

1. c	**6.** a	**11.** c	**16.** c	**21.** d
2. a	**7.** c	**12.** b	**17.** a	**22.** a
3. d	**8.** c	**13.** b	**18.** b	**23.** c
4. a	**9.** a	**14.** e	**19.** d	**24.** d
5. a	**10.** c	**15.** b	**20.** a	**25.** C, B, D, A

Part IV

GLOSSARY OF TERMS

ABAFT THE BEAM—Any direction between broad on the beam and astern.

ABEAM—At right angles to the ship's keel.

AFT—Near, toward, or at the stern of a craft.

AGROUND—Resting or lodged on the bottom.

ALTER COURSE—A change in course.

ANCHORAGE—An area where a vessel anchors or may anchor, either because of suitability or designation.

APPROACHING—Manner of advance.

ARC—A part of a curved line, as of a circle.

ASTERN—Bearing approximately 180 degrees relative. The opposite is ahead.

BEAM—The vessel's extreme breadth of a ship.

BELL—A device for producing a distinctive sound by the vibration of a hollow, cup-shaped metallic instrument which gives forth a ringing sound when struck.

BOUNDARY LINES—Detailed lines established dividing the high seas from rivers, harbors and inland waters. Inland and Pilot Rules apply inside these lines; International Rules apply outside these lines. See Figs. 1, 2, 3, 4 and 5.

BOW—The forward part of a ship, craft, or aircraft.

BUOY—A floating object, other than a lightship, moored or anchored to the bottom as an aid to navigation.

BURDENED VESSEL—A vessel which is required to keep out of the way of a privileged vessel.

CHANNEL—That part of a body of water deep enough for navigation through an area otherwise not suitable. It is usually marked by a single or double line of buoys and sometimes by ranges.

CLOSE ABOARD—Very near.

CLOSEHAULED—Sailing close to the wind.

CROSS SIGNALS—Illegal signals; that is, answering one blast with two or two blasts with one.

DANGER SIGNALS—(International Rules) At least five short and rapid blasts on the whistle.
(Inland Rules) Not less than four short and rapid blasts of the steam whistle.

DEAD AHEAD—Bearing 000 degrees relative.

DOCK—The slip or waterways between two piers, or cut into the land for the berthing of ships.

DREDGE—A water craft used to dredge an area.

ENGAGED IN FISHING—Fishing with nets, lines, or trawls but does not include fishing with trolling lines.

FAIRWAY—The main traveled part of a waterway; a marine thoroughfare.

FIXED LIGHT—A light having constant luminous intensity.

FLARE-UP LIGHT—Any bright white light conspicuously displayed, used to attract attention.

FLOATING PLANT—Dredges, derrick boats, snag boats, drill boats, pile drivers, maneuver boats, hydraulic graders, survey boats, working barges, working in navigable channels.

FOG BANK—Mass of fog observed at a distance, most commonly at sea.

FOG SIGNAL—A device that transmits a warning signal by a vessel or aid to navigation during low visibility.

FOREMAST—Forward mast of a vessel.

FORWARD—In a direction nearer dead ahead; toward the bow.

GENERAL PRUDENTIAL RULE—Rule 27 and Article 27 of the International and Inland Rules, respectively. Rule 27: "In obeying and construing these Rules, due regard shall be had to all dangers of navigation and collision, and to any special circumstances, including the limitations of the craft involved, which may render a departure from the above Rules necessary in order to avoid immediate danger." Article 27 does not include the phrase "including the limitations of the craft involved."

GONG—A flat disk-shaped or saucerlike bell.

GROUND—To touch bottom or run aground.

GROUNDING—The touching of the bottom by a vessel.

HEIGHT ABOVE THE HULL—Height above the uppermost continuous deck.

HORN—A device for producing a distinctive sound, and consisting of a tube with a cross section varying in size.

INLAND RULES OF THE ROAD—Rules to be followed by all vessels while navigating upon inland waters of the United States.

INTERNATIONAL RULES OF THE ROAD—The International Regulations for Preventing Collisions at Sea.

MADE FAST—Secured to or tied to, as a line made fast to a cleat.

MAKING WAY—Progress through the water.

MASTHEAD—Uppermost part of a mast.

MASTHEAD LIGHT—A bright white light so constructed on or in front of the foremast, or if a vessel without a foremast then in the forepart of the vessel, so constructed as to show an unbroken light over an arc of the horizon of 20 points of the compass (225 degrees), so fixed as to show the light 10 points (112-1/2 degrees) on each side of the vessel; that is, from right ahead to 2 points (22-1/2 degrees), abaft the beam on either side, and of such a character as to be visible at a distance of at least 5 miles.

MODERATE SPEED—That speed which will enable a vessel proceeding in restricted visibility to stop in one half the distance of visibility.

MOTORBOAT ACT OF 1940—An Act to amend laws for preventing collisions of vessels, to regulate the equipment of certain motorboats on the navigable waters of the United States, and for other purposes.

MOTORBOAT—(As used in the Motorboat Act of 1940). Any boat propelled by machinery and not more than 65 feet in length with the exception of tugs propelled by steam.

MOTORBOAT CLASSES—(As subject to the Act of 1940)

Class A. Less than sixteen feet in length.

Class 1. Sixteen feet or over and less than twenty-six feet in length.

Class 2. Twenty-six feet or over and less than forty feet in length.

Class 3. Forty feet or over and not more than sixty-five feet in length.

MOORINGS—Chains, bridles, anchors, etc., used in securing a craft to the ground.

NAVIGABLE WATERS OF THE U.S.—Those waters of the United States, including the territorial sea adjacent thereto, the general character of which is navigable, and which, either by themselves or by uniting with other waters, form a continuous waterway on which boats or vessels may navigate or travel between two or more States, or to or from foreign nations.

OVERTAKING—A vessel coming up with another vessel from any direction more than 22-1/2 degrees (2 points) abaft her beam.

PILOT—A person who has extensive knowledge of channels, aids to navigation, dangers to navigation, of a particular area and is licensed to direct the movements of a vessel; as through pilot waters.

PILOT VESSEL—A small vessel used by a pilot to go to or from a vessel employing his services.

PORT SIDE—The left side of a vessel facing forward.

PORT SIDE LIGHT—A red light so constructed as to show an unbroken light over an arc of the horizon of 112-1/2 degrees (10 points of the compass), so fixed as to show the light from ahead to 22-1/2 degrees (2 points) abaft the beam on the port side, and of such a character as to be visible at a distance of at least 2 miles.

PORT TACK—The mainsail is carried so that the tack of the sail is to port of the clew.

POWER-DRIVEN VESSEL—Any vessel propelled by machinery; every vessel under power, whether under sail or not, is to be considered a power-driven vessel.

PROLONGED BLAST—A blast of from four to six seconds' duration.

RUNNING—A point of sail in which the wind is coming from astern.

RUNNING LIGHTS—Navigation lights.

RECIPROCAL—A direction 180° from a given direction.

SEAPLANE—A flying boat and any other aircraft designed to maneuver on the water.

SEAWAY—Headway of a vessel. A shipping lane.

SHORT BLAST—A blast of the whistle, about one second duration.

SPECIAL CIRCUMSTANCES—Applies to Rule and Article 27 International and Inland Rules, known as the General Prudential Rule and Sec. 80.11 of the Pilot Rules. Also Rule and Article 29 known as the Rule of Good Seamanship.

SPUDS—See Moorings.

STARBOARD SIDE—The right side of a vessel facing forward.

STARBOARD TACK—When the mainsail is carried so that the tack of the sail is to starboard of the clew.

STEAM VESSEL—(Inland and Pilot Rules) Any vessel propelled by machinery.

STEERAGEWAY—The condition in which a ship has sufficient way on that it will respond to rudder movements to maintain a desired course.

STERN LIGHT—A white light carried on the stern of a vessel so constructed that it shall show an unbroken light over an arc of the horizon of 135 degrees (12 points of the compass), so fixed as to show the light 67-1/2 degrees (6 points) from right aft on each side of the vessel, and of such a character as to be visible at a distance of at least 2 miles.

TRAWLING—Fishing by dragging on the bottom a bag-shaped net.

TROLLING—Pulling a line through the water with its lure and hook.

VESSEL—Any type of craft, except aircraft, which can be used for transportation through water.

VISIBILITY—The extreme horizontal distance at which prominent objects can be seen and identified by the unaided eye.

WHISTLE—Any appliance capable of producing the prescribed short and prolonged blasts.

APPENDIX

APPENDIX

COAST GUARD OFFICES — MARINE INSPECTION

The United States Coast Guard is the authority for issuing deck officers' licenses. Each Coast Guard District Commander is provided with an Officer in Charge, Marine Inspection, to furnish license renewal forms and questions that must be answered on the Rules of the Road applicable for the waters for which the applicant is licensed.

Following is a list of the offices of the Officers in Charge, Marine Inspection.

1st Coast Guard District

447 Commercial St., Boston, Massachusetts 02109
P.O. Box 108, Pearl Street Station, Portland, Maine 04112
409 Federal Bldg., Providence, Rhode Island 02903

2nd Coast Guard District

Federal Bldg., 1520 Market St., St. Louis, Missouri 63103
P.O. Box 391, Cairo, Illinois 62914
Box 695, Dubuque, Iowa 62914
Room 8413, Federal Office Bldg., 550 Main St., Cincinnati, Ohio 4520
254 Francis Bldg., 4th and Chestnut Sts., Louisville, Kentucky 40202
856 Federal Bldg., 167 No. Main St., Memphis, Tennessee 38103
670 U.S. Court House, 801 Broadway, Nashville, Tennessee 37203
1215 Park Bldg., Pittsburgh, Pennsylvania 15222
328 Post Office and Federal Court House Bldg., 5th Ave., and 9th St., Huntington, West Virginia 25701

3rd Coast Guard District

720 Custom House, New York, New York 10004
302 Post Office Bldg., New London, Connecticut 06321
313 Federal Bldg., Albany, New York 12207
Custom House, Philadelphia, Pennsylvania 19106

5th Coast Guard District

Federal Bldg., Room 202, Portsmouth, Virginia 23705
Room 101-105 Custom House, Wilmington, North Carolina 28401
Custom House, Baltimore, Maryland 21233

7th Coast Guard District

Room 1202, Federal Bldg., 51 S.W. 1st Ave., Miami, Florida 33130
316 Franklin St., P.O. Box 3172, Tampa, Florida 33601
32 Custom House, Charleston, South Carolina 29401
P.O. Box 191, Savannah, Georgia 31402
210 Federal Bldg., P.O. Box 4968, Jacksonville, Florida 32201
P.O. Box 3666, 302 Federal Bldg., San Juan, Puerto Rico 00904

8th Coast Guard District

310 Custom House, 423 Canal St., New Orleans, Louisiana 70130
563 Federal Bldg., Mobile, Alabama 36602
General Delivery, Port Arthur, Texas 77641
232 Custom House, Galveston, Texas 77550
101 Federal Bldg., Corpus Christi, Texas 78401
7300 Wingate St., Houston, Texas 77011

9th Coast Guard District

1055 East 9th St., Cleveland, Ohio 44114
440 Federal Bldg., 121 Ellicott St., Buffalo, New York 14203
205 Federal Bldg., Oswego, New York 13126
424 Federal Bldg., Detroit, Michigan 48226
311 Federal Bldg., Duluth, Minnesota 55802
Federal Bldg., 234 Summit St., Toledo, Ohio 43604
Municipal Bldg., Saint Ignace, Michigan 49781
10101 South Ewing Ave., Chicago, Illinois 60617
National Bank Bldg., Ludington, Michigan 49431
Room 400, 135 West Wells St., Milwaukee, Wisconsin 53203

11th Coast Guard District

300 So. Ferry St., San Pedro, California 90731
Room 12A, Broadway Pier, San Diego, California 92101

12th Coast Guard District

Station B., Box 2029, San Francisco, California 94126

13th Coast Guard District

618 2nd Ave., Seattle, Washington 98104
202 Lincoln Bldg., 208 S.W. 5th Ave., Portland, Oregon 97204

14th Coast Guard District

610 Fort St., Honolulu, Hawaii 96813
Marianas, Guam

17th Coast Guard District

P.O. Box 2631, Juneau, Alaska 99801
P.O. Box 1286 Anchorage, Alaska 99501